Lizzie Jones

S★B

Published in 2014 by:

Stellar Books LLP
Dunham Gatehouse
Charcoal Road,
Bowdon
Cheshire,
WA14 4RY
UK

ISBN: 978-1910275023

A copy of this book is available in the British Library.

Typeset and edited by Patricia C Byron of Stellar Books LLP.
www.stellarbooks.co.uk

Front and rear covers designed by Nikki Griffiths of Tinker and Faff.
www.tinkerandfaff.com

FSC® is a non-profit international organisation established to promote responsible management of the world's forests. Products carrying the FSC® label are independently certified to assure consumers that they come from forests that are managed to meet the social economic and ecological needs of present and future generations.

For Dan

To the moon and back

CONTENTS

Acknowledgements

Years ago, when I first decided to sit down and write this book, I jokingly said that, by the time it finally got to print – if it ever did – the list of acknowledgements would be almost as long as the book itself and at the time it was true. But like so many things in life, you soon find out who your true friends are and who really cares enough about what you're doing to stick it out until the bitter end. So, as a result, the list is considerably shorter than I first thought it would be, but I now know it contains *the* most important people, without whom there would be no book to read.

I want to stress there's no particular order of importance here; everyone mentioned knows where they fit into the whole scheme of things and that's all that matters at the end of the day.

My publisher Patsy Byron is an incredibly inspirational lady and she's been fabulous at getting me to pull my finger out and finally get this finished by giving me endless advice and encouragement. It was so reassuring to know I could trust her implicitly to do what she does best to make sure the book made it into print.

Thank you Susan Leigh. Firstly for planting the seed that led me to Patsy and Stellar Books when this all began and secondly, and perhaps more importantly, for being so strong and supportive and so very, very wise. I couldn't have asked for a better sounding board and I'm so lucky to be able to count you as a friend.

There is no doubt that the book wouldn't look as good as it does without the amazing talent of Nikki Griffiths of Tinker & Faff, compulsive doodler and graphic designer extraordinaire, who showed infinite patience throughout the whole process, particularly given that I'm most definitely the client from hell. Nikki, you are a star and have been such an inspiration ever since I first started this journey. I'll always be grateful for the time and energy you've given so selflessly.

I need to give a special mention to the lovely Lisa Wood, who's also stuck with me through all of this. You know me better than most and the personal struggles I've been through to get this far and you've always been there to encourage me. You of all people understand why this is so important to me and your unfailing enthusiasm has carried me along when the words wouldn't come. You're right – this is my destiny.

I've known Gill Cronshaw and Lesley Cox since our children were small and they were the first of many to get involved and write their own lists. Thank you ladies for putting up with my endless insecurities over the years and always being there with coffee and wine when I needed it. No one could ask for better friends.

And last but by no means least, Mike, who has been part of my life for over half of that life. You have stood by me through thick and thin and, without you, none of this would ever have come about. Thank you for all you've done and all you've given me over the years, I am eternally grateful.

1

WHAT IT'S ALL ABOUT

When did we start living our lives at one hundred miles an hour? When did it all become like the film of the same name - all fast and furious? We always seem to be in a hurry, permanently rushing from place to place and task to task. We're constantly trying to keep up as life seems to be escaping us. Sometimes it feels like running to stand still; we keep going faster, but it's never quite fast enough to keep up with everything. It so often feels like life is just passing us by.

Our days are generally filled with work and responsibility and commitment and because we spend so much time doing the things we have to do, there never seems to be enough time to do the things we really want to. Sure, we manage to keep up with work and the *really* important stuff, but there never seems to be any time left over for anything else. And what are all these things we're doing? Well, certainly not the things we'd actually *like* to be doing. How many times do you hear yourself or someone else saying "I'd rather be…….." or "I wish I was…..."?

Unfortunately, for most of us, the need to make a living, pay the mortgage – in some cases just survive financially – means we have to spend most of our waking hours working. Sad, but true. Then, when we're not working, there are so many other demands on our time – cooking, cleaning, shopping, ironing, the garden, not to mention the endless taxi service for the kids, to football matches and swimming lessons and ballet and…… the list of things we feel we have to do just goes on and on and on. And when all that's done, we often feel so drained by the effort we have had to put into getting through it that we can't find the energy to do anything else and spend night after night slumped in front of the television or, as I'm sure has happened to all of us at some time in the not too distant past, fast asleep on the sofa.

Then, at the end of the day, we drag ourselves off to bed and when we wake up the next morning, the same old routine kicks in again and weeks go by without us doing anything apart from "working". In other words, what little time we do get away from our place of work or business quite often passes us by without anything remotely remarkable happening, because we just don't seem to have the time to do anything else. Basically, our batteries are continually running down and if we don't find ways of re-charging them, before we know it we're running out of energy. I'm guessing we've all seen the battery advert with the cute little bunny, endlessly charging about even when everything around it has run out of power? Unfortunately, we don't have an inexhaustible supply of energy; our batteries won't last long enough to enable us to go on indefinitely.

And we're not just short of time during the week. Because most of Monday to Friday is taken up with work, we always try to cram everything else we have to do into the weekend. Because we've been so busy during the week, we feel the need to spend all weekend doing the housework, shopping, cooking, cleaning and ferrying the kids to every activity imaginable. So what we are doing, effectively, is spending all the weekend working too. We're essentially doing the same sort of thing we do Monday to Friday, it's just the surroundings have changed.

How many of us have promised to make up for all this exhausting behaviour by having some "down-time" at the weekend, only to find that, on Sunday evening, we still didn't pause for breath and we really don't know where the last two days went, because there's nothing out of the ordinary to remember them by? Hardly surprising when all they consisted of was the same old stuff we seem to spend every weekend doing. So then when Monday morning comes around, we go back to work feeling just as jaded as we did when we left it behind on Friday evening. We've had no rest, no respite, no variety and before we know it, we feel like time is passing us by in a whirl of work, commitments and struggle. Without us realising how it happened, life has become a treadmill we can neither stop nor get off.

This could possibly sound all too familiar and if you're reading this and thinking "Oh that feels just like my life" then don't be too hard on yourself. Firstly, you're not alone, we all do it (not that it makes it right, of course) and secondly, don't worry, reading this book can start to change all that by helping you make the most of your time off and showing you how to get more out of your life in all sorts of tiny little ways. Now I can already hear some of you saying that all this is fine in theory, but you simply don't have the time but, I can assure you, reading this book will help you realise that we can all make time for stuff we really want to do and we all have far more free time than we realise. The real problem is we're just not very good at making the most of it. Relax, we're not talking big stuff here – the best *52 Lists* are full of things that can be done in half a day or less. And everyone can find time to do that if they really put their mind to it.

Many years ago, my mum sat me down for a heart-to-heart. She was concerned that I'd been doing far too much, not least of which was working long hours and not taking any time for me and, although I hated to admit it at the time, she was right, I hadn't. I was a single mum, holding down a full-time job and trying to juggle work, the home and childcare. In reality, though, I wasn't doing anything out of the ordinary in today's fast-paced world. There are hundreds of thousands of us doing the same, week in, week out, working too hard and trying to cram 28 hours of activity into a 24 hour day; basically, just coping with life in general. When she'd finished talking, she handed me a box. It was small and black and on the top, in bold white letters, it said "Never be too busy making a living that you forget to make a life" and I realised it was her way of telling me to take a big step back and think about doing things differently. You see, it's easy to think that, by working hard and providing for those who depend on us, we're doing a good thing and we are. But, and here's the crucial bit, by doing all of that we're forgetting the real reason why we do it at all and that is supposed to be trying to make a better life. Because what on earth is the point of working all those hours if we never get any pleasure out of what it provides? We work to live, after all, not the other way around, but it's hard to remember that when we're always on the go, one hundred miles an hour, never stopping to catch our breath.

Now, I realise that not all of us have such busy lives. There are just as many people out there who have exactly the opposite; that is to say they have little or nothing to do every day. However, before you all start saying how much you'd like a life like that, just stop to think how dull it would be if you had nothing of any consequence to do day in, day out, with nothing to work towards and nothing of any significance to look forward to?

Some of you reading this might *think* that sounds like nirvana but believe me, it would wear thin after a while. Face it, there's only so much you can do around the house before it's all been done, and then, with nothing at all to occupy your time, every day must seem stretch into an eternity of emptiness. You'd soon find life lacked purpose and direction because, with so much time to fill, it's easy to spend great big chunks of it doing nothing, literally nothing and then complacency and inactivity set in and the less you do, the less you feel motivated to do and that can be just as big a problem as being endlessly busy. Yes, really, it can and some of you reading this will be more than familiar with this feeling, when the days seem all too long and there's simply not enough to do to fill them. A life without stimulation can be very dull indeed.

So, whether we're too busy or not busy enough, most of us feel, at one time or another, that there's something missing in our lives. We either want to do more, or we need to do less, but few of us are altogether satisfied with our lot. And if you're not happy with your life, you need to do something to change it.

The 52 List is all about change. Ask yourself this; how much better would you feel if every week you got to spend time doing something you really wanted to do? Something fun, something that makes you feel better about yourself and about life in general? Because spending time doing things that make us happy, improves our lives. And feeling happy means every day can be more satisfying, lighter, less stressful and increases our overall sense of wellbeing. In short, happiness makes life worth living.

And that's essentially what this book is all about – helping you make more out of the life you have and I'm going to show you that it's not that difficult, if you just put in a little effort.

Now, I have to stress at this point that the way in which *The 52 List* can bring about change is not earth-shattering. Reading this book won't necessarily change your life remarkably, although you never know, it just might. I doubt very much whether it will make you rich, although I suppose it could – you never know what possibilities might come your way when you're not even looking. Unfortunately, it won't make you thin, but that's definitely a possible side-effect because you'll be so busy getting on with enjoying your life, there'll be less time to sit around eating just for the sake of it! However, what I can promise it will do is help you to feel like you've genuinely done something important. It will make you feel happier. What it will do is help you realise you've achieved something fantastic; nothing radical or life-changing, but which will make your life better, richer and more fulfilled. If you follow what I've set out in *The 52 List* you'll end up having some new experiences, which in turn will create some great memories. It will fill you with joy and excitement and it *will* improve your life in more ways than you can imagine. And surely that's what life should be all about?

Now *The 52 List* process isn't hard. Really, it isn't. All you need to do is follow the rules set out over the following chapters and you'll end up broadening your horizons, meeting new people and, hopefully, re-building relationships. OK, I appreciate you might find it difficult to start off with, that you will have to spend some time in deep thought and that getting it right will take conscious effort on your part, but if you do it properly, I can guarantee it'll be worth every minute of time you invest in it.

The whole point of this book is to start changing your life for the better and showing you that the author Kurt Vonnegut was right all along, when he said "Enjoy the little things in life, because one day you will look back and realise they were the big things"

So let's get started………

2

How it all Began......

This first bit is slightly sexist, so I apologise, in advance, to any men reading this book to whom the next sentence also applies. Back in the mid-nineties, I became a mum and like many other women before me, I decided I wanted to stay at home after my baby was born. This is where the apology comes in – there are many men who decide to stop working when they become a dad, so if you're a man who has taken this life-changing step and given it all up to be a house-husband, please assume all of the following applies to you too and just change the gender where appropriate, if you wouldn't mind? Thanks!

Before I decided I wanted to have children I had a career; well-paid, challenging, but, most importantly, fulltime. I was working on average 40-50 hours per week and was climbing the professional ladder steadily and enjoying every minute. But I stress the word "had" because, when my husband and I decided we wanted to start a family, I chose to give up that career and be a housewife.

Both Mike and I grew up in the North East of England in the sixties. This was an area of the country where the sense of community was strong and most of the people we grew up with were brought up by members of the extended family unit. In our cases, our day to day care came from our grandparents. We both had parents who worked full-time – and working hours were generally longer then – and from breakfast in the morning until bath time at night, our grandparents took care of us. It also has to be acknowledged that professional child-care wasn't as widespread back then as it is today but all that aside, it was just the way it was done. Feeling we'd benefitted from this close family bond, we dearly wanted to bring up our own son the same way, but as I'd long since moved away from my parents and my in-laws worked full-time, there were no available grandparents to take on the role of full-time carer.

So it was decided I would give up work and become a full-time mum, for at least a year or two and that's what I did and, in reality, was quite glad of the change of pace...... at first. I threw myself into housewife mode with enthusiasm. I cooked, cleaned, shopped, washed and ironed. I fulfilled the role of a stay at home mum admirably; my husband always had a clean shirt to wear and came home to a home-cooked meal every night. The house was clean and tidy, and my son spent care-free days filled with toddler clubs and swimming and trips to the park.

Don't get me wrong, I realise this was an incredible privilege in so many ways – not everyone is fortunate enough to be sufficiently financially secure to enable them to do this and I am eternally grateful to Mike for giving me the opportunity to stay at home. I will always look back on it as one of the best times of my life. But it did have its disadvantages, one of which was I felt like I was no longer in control of my own destiny. Every day I was surrounded by lots of little people and, even when there were other adults around, the conversation always seemed to be about children and potty-training and development and basically all things baby-related. OK, so I didn't exactly want to have a conversation about quantum physics, but used to the stimulation of conversation on such subjects as finance, politics and current affairs, I found my brain was slowly sliding into inactivity and I developed the feeling that I'd ceased to exist as a fully functioning member of the adult community. Everything I did, everything I got to talk about, seemed to revolve around children and I got very tired of everyone referring to me as a "mummy". In a very short space of time, it appeared that I'd completely lost my own identity.

So, there I was, the year after my son was born, sitting down in that quiet lull between Christmas and New Year feeling strangely bereft. It suddenly occurred to me that over twelve months of my life had passed by and I genuinely felt I had nothing to show for it. I know this might sound ridiculous to some, but I'd had a high-powered job and was used to being in control and making things happen and generally being in the thick of things. Now my life seemed so small and insignificant and that I didn't seem to exist except as an extension of my son. Please don't get me wrong, I don't regret having a baby for one minute. I can't possibly imagine my life without this perfect extension of myself being part of it. I know that having him is the most important single thing I've ever done and I feel eternally blessed, but at that point in time, I suddenly failed to see why on earth I had decided to give up my former life and I couldn't feel any genuine sense of achievement. My husband, bless him, took me by the hand and pointed at our darling boy, 15 months old, happily pulling chocolate ornaments off the Christmas tree and stuffing them in his face, foil wrapper and all and tried to explain that I had been so busy raising our child that I could be forgiven for not having done much else. Ha! That didn't placate me in the slightest. I was a captain of industry (OK, not exactly, but I was used to wielding a bit of power here and there!) and raising a small, happy go lucky, adorable child just wasn't enough. "But what have I really done?" I wailed, "What? Show me!" So he pointed to our son and said

"See—right there, there's your achievement". "No, not enough!" I said, "I need more."

If I'd actually sat down and thought about it rationally, I'd have realised quite quickly that I hadn't exactly been sitting around on my (still slightly chunky) backside whiling away my time watching daytime TV or gossiping with like-minded mums at the local playground, but I did feel like I should have had more to show for my year off. I really felt like I'd let myself down.

I couldn't put my finger on precisely what the problem was, to be honest. My son was happy, healthy and well-balanced. The house was, mostly, clean and tidy. The washing and ironing were done, the fridge was always full. As a housewife and stay at home mum, I'd fulfilled the brief perfectly. So far so good. So what was the problem? Simply that I felt there had to be more. I couldn't get away from the feeling there should be some points of reference to my year off, something to show for all the time that had slipped past me while I was wrapped up in being Supermum. Something I could look back on and remember. Something to bring on a warm fuzzy feeling in years to come…..

I carried the feeling of gloom around with me for days. What the hell had I done, I kept asking myself. Surely there had to be something more to show for all those hours when my baby was sleeping, or playing, or hanging out with all the other toddlers? But I still couldn't work out exactly what was bugging me so much. Why the heck was I so dissatisfied with my lot?

And then, in a quiet moment on a day when the house was empty and still and I was slopping around the house feeling like I had nothing to do, it dawned on me. Just like that, it struck me that all the time I'd been doing stuff and keeping myself busy, I'd been driven by the desire to keep everyone else happy. Sure, my baby was thriving, Mike had everything he needed; I'd pandered to their every want, satisfied every demand. Unfortunately, the one thing I'd failed to think about was what I might need. It had never occurred to me to do anything for myself. While I'd been so busy looking after everyone else, I'd totally forgotten to look after me. OK, I was healthy enough physically, it wasn't that. No, I had neglected myself mentally. Gone was the stimulation I'd got while I was working away at my career, gone was the stuff that taxed my brain, that got the grey matter working. The problem was, I'd given up all the mental stimulation that work had given me and I hadn't come up with anything else to take its place. When I made the decision to go on indefinite maternity leave, all I'd effectively done was swap one job for another, except my new job wasn't mentally challenging enough. I used to work in an office, now I worked at home. I was essentially doing the same as I had before, only in a different way. And it wasn't making me happy.

I began to understand that what I really needed was to put me first every once in a while, rather than focussing totally on everyone else. It was just as important to spend time on things I actually wanted to do rather than the things I had to do, things that I could take pleasure in, and therefore feel a sense of achievement having completed. Let's be honest, a basket of ironing isn't exactly inspiring, is it? Don't get me wrong, I didn't actually mind doing it, but at the end of the day it was just another job to knock off the to-do-list, something that had to be done as part of my job description. Where was the life-enriching stuff that creates a lasting impression on your brain and in your heart? I realised that, in years to come, no one would remember that I'd always got all the ironing done. Imagine that one on your grave stone – "Well, her ironing basket was always empty".   I also realised that I'd been living my life in the way I thought others would approve of and admire; a big part of my attitude and approach was clearly driven by how it looked to others. Foolishly, I'd thought it mattered how I would be judged as a mother and a wife and I realised, yet again, that I'd got my priorities all wrong. I mean, when the kids are all grown up, will they REALLY remember that you always got their tea ready on time, or that their school uniform was the neatest or cleanest in the whole school? Of course not. I'm actually laughing as I type thinking how ridiculous that sounds now but, at the time, being the perfect wife and mother seemed to be all about getting that sort of pointless stuff achieved. Fortunately, I saw the light back then too and realised I had to give my life more meaning and create something which I could look back on and feel proud. I acknowledged that I had to start changing my priorities and creating something more enduring than clean windows and a well-stocked freezer.

I know, I thought. I'll write a list of things I actually *want* to do and that might give me some impetus to start changing the status quo. Surprisingly, making that decision was the easy bit; deciding on how to go about it proved to be far more difficult. I had no idea where to start. So I sat down and did what we often do when we need inspiration these days; I went on the internet.

As I started sifting through all the information out there – and boy, was there *a lot*! – I came across so many versions of essentially the same thing and it didn't take me long to realise that lists of things people want to do are all over the World Wide Web. However, as I started reading some of them, I realised just as quickly that there was nothing there I could apply to my own life. You know the sort of list I mean, that includes such things as riding on an elephant and trekking to Machu Picchu. How the heck was I going to be able to do any of those things? Don't get me wrong; in the whole scheme of things they're all amazing things and I wouldn't be averse to doing any of them, but there's two big problems with those sort of lists for the majority of us. Firstly, they tend to cost a whole load of money. Now, as I'd already managed to persuade my husband to work incredibly hard to give me the luxury of being able to stay at home, I couldn't see me being able to convince him to part with anything even remotely resembling the vast amount of cash doing even one of the ideas on the list would take, so that was a non-starter. Secondly, it's not like you can decide to go to Peru on a whim and be back in time for tea. You can't just wake up on Monday morning and think hmmm... fancy a trip to Peru, dear? No, big things take lots of time and, quite frankly, who has it? And this was, and still is for most people, the big problem; time. There's never enough of it. I mean, seriously, when we're struggling to get through what we *have* to do, where on earth are we going to find weeks on end to go to far flung places or anything else on our "lists of things to do before we die" for that matter? No, I decided, there had to be a different way of feeling fulfilled. A way that didn't involve enormous amounts of time and cash and that we could just decide to do at the drop of a hat.

While I was thinking about it, everyone else seemed to be talking about resolutions, things they wanted to get done in the next 12 months and how difficult they were to stick to and I realised that therein lay another problem. Resolutions are all very well, but they're not really achievable for most of us because we set ourselves tasks we *think* we want to do rather than what we *actually* want to do. The most common resolution is probably to lose weight, but let's be honest, how many of us have made that resolution and actually stuck to it, never mind achieved our goal? None that I know of. Why? Because it's too hard. We start the year with all good intentions and then after three or four weeks, we get bored and let our resolve weaken and we have a biscuit with our morning coffee and we realise how much we've missed biscuits and so we start having them again. Not too many, you understand, just one or two, now and again. Oh, and an occasional piece of cake – because one piece won't hurt, will it? And then there's an extra potato with dinner – because it was only a little one – and before we know it, the weight starts to creep back on again and then we wake up one morning and get back on the scales and realise we're right back where we started and another resolution bites the dust. Well, until Lent, that is, when we may give it another go, but rarely is this any more successful. Been there, done that! Now there are real reasons why this doesn't work, but we're not going to go into them here – that's a whole book of its own! Suffice it to say we're setting ourselves totally unachievable goals in an incredibly unrealistic time frame and when we don't succeed, as so few of us do, we're just more despondent than ever and, worse still, we feel like we've failed when, realistically, we'd set ourselves up for it right from the start.

So, bucket lists weren't the answer, nor were resolutions. So, what was? As it turns out, the solution was blindingly obvious. As I struggled to work out how I was going to go about getting my list together, I realised that if I left out all the things that caused these sort of lists to remain unfulfilled, I stood a chance of getting it right. So, rather than trying to work out a list of what things on my list *should* be, I wrote down all the things they *shouldn't* be and it didn't take me long to come up with the following: expensive, time-consuming, unrealistic and endless. If these were the things that prevented things getting done, surely if I avoided them or, did the complete opposite, then I stood a chance of getting a decent list together. This was actually a much better plan, I decided, and set about making a list of "things to do" that were inexpensive, quick and very much results driven, that is, at the end of whatever time you spent on them, however short, you could clearly see what you'd achieved. Sorted!

And so my list slowly started to take shape and before too long it was full of little, seemingly unremarkable things, but all of which I'd been wanting to do for some time. And the list just grew and grew. The more I wrote, the more inspiration I got and the more I realised that there were literally dozens of things I'd been ignoring that were actually what I really *wanted* to do. And as the list grew, the more enthusiastic I got and before I knew it, I decided to try to get 52 things written on my list. Why? Because then, when I sat down at the same time the following year and reflected on the last twelve months of my life, I'd realise that I'd achieved a whole lot, even if I only managed to do one little thing every week. Because, I decided, who the heck can't find enough time for themselves once, just once, every week and, as some of the things I wanted to do would be far more enjoyable if I didn't do them alone, I was actually helping to create some fun for those around me: my family, my friends, the people who were really important to me.

And so *The 52 List* was born. Just a list, nothing too startling, but the things I'd put on it were so important to me that I realised if I sat down in twelve months' time to ponder where my life had gone, I'd have no one to blame but myself for not making the time to make my life better.

I was so proud of my list of things I really wanted to do. Not big things, not "bucket list" things, but little things. Things I knew would make a difference to my life but, more importantly, which I could fit into my daily routine. Things that would give me a sense of achievement and start to re-connect me to my friends and the life I had BC (Before Children). I already knew that the next year would be different, that I would get to the same point twelve months hence and look back over my year with a smile, having achieved some personal goals and with a head (and a box) full of memories; 52 things to look forward to, 52 things to look back on, all with, I hoped, lots of laughter, maybe some tears, but certainly a smile or several. And it did make a difference, that year, and the next and the next and I liked it so much I shared the idea with friends and they all liked it and I realised that this was something that was very much worth sharing. So I wrote it all down and now here you are, reading all about it so you can go off and do it too.

The idea of this book is very simple, therefore; to explain the whys and wherefores of *The 52 List*, the reasons why you should be doing this for yourself and advice on how you can get it to work for you. I'll take you through the background and the psychology, albeit home spun, of the importance of the list, rules on what your should and, more importantly should not, think about putting on your list and how to keep a permanent record of it for posterity so that, in years to come, you can look back on and re-visit some incredibly happy memories. Most importantly, it's all about sharing the happiness with friends and family and those who mean the most to you, to spread the joy and make everyone's life just a little bit better. I know it's a very small thing, but even the tiniest light is welcome when you're in the dark and I always think of my *52 List* things as my little spots of sunshine, even in the depths of winter.

The good thing about *The 52 List* is that once you've worked out how to get started and then how to go about writing your list, the hard part is over. But, if you do it right, even the writing of the list itself should fill you with joy and happy anticipation of all the things you've got to look forward to in the future. It really can become life-changing. Yes, really, it can! The only person who's stopping you from making your life better is you! You have the power to change things and get that list started so that every year you can have a whole host of wonderful things to look forward to.

My friends have been saying "You finally written *The 52 List*? About time too!" You see I have to admit that this book has been many, many years in the writing, having been shelved, postponed and neglected numerous times. It is only the encouragement and support of those same friends that has actually got me this far and spurred me on to finally get it all written down and out there so anyone who wants to can give it a go. If only I could have put "write *The 52 List* book" on my own *52 List* it might have got done much sooner but, unfortunately, as you'll find out as you read on, or maybe you've already worked out from this chapter, it simply doesn't qualify, because of the sheer commitment of time it's taken to get it to this point. But you know what? None of that matters right now, because it's written, it's published and, most importantly of all, I got there eventually!

3

52 SOUNDS LIKE A HECK

OF A LOT!

This book is called *The 52 List*, so you'd be right in assuming that the title comes from the fact that your list has 52 things on it. Hmmm….. bit of a no-brainer that one! But I can also imagine that, at this point, a good many of you are thinking "That's a lot of things." You'd also be right; it is, an awful lot.

When I started to write this book, I did some digging to see whether the number 52 had any particular significance and I realised that it crops up all over the place – in history, in theology and in all sorts of literature and poetry, but, in all honesty, there's no real mystical or spiritual relevance to the number. There are 52 white keys on a standard piano, there are 52 cards in a pack. The ancient Mayans divided time into periods of 52 years and awaited the end of the world on the last day of every 52nd year. Sorry, that's the closest I could get to any sort of facts that had relevance to the number, so I'm going with the obvious; there are 52 weeks in a year. And because there are 52 weeks in a year, if you have 52 things on your list and only do one thing a week for that year, at the end of it you'll have a very long list of achievements to look back on. Simple. Well, not quite that simple, but not far off. Really, there's no need to overthink this.

Before you all start saying you can't possibly come up with that many things, just take a moment to think about it and you'll be genuinely surprised how quickly your list starts to grow. I know 52 different things sounds unachievable and you're right, it most probably is, *if* you try to do it all in one go. But there's nothing at all to stop you writing your list over a period of time. There's no real problem in starting the list with just a few things and then adding more as you go along. My own personal experience has shown that it's actually quite difficult at first to come up with 52 "things" if you follow the rules for what can and what can't go on the list (see later), so if you struggle to come up with that many, don't worry, that's OK.

After I'd been doing my own list for a few years, I shared the idea with friends who liked it and wanted to join in, but were initially put off by the idea that it should be so long. So I convinced them to give it a go anyway and one or two of them decided to start off with a list of just twelve things. Now come on, surely we can all manage that? I defy anyone to say they can't come up with at least twelve different things. It's only one a month, after all. One a month! How hard can that be? And if you really can't come up with twelve things, why not start off with six. Let's be honest, any number will do, but I always like to start off by trying to find all 52 and then when I run out of ideas, I stop. But then I keep the list lying around where I can see it every day, and every time I get another idea, I add it to the list and before I know it, I'm nearly there.

It's nowhere near as difficult as it sounds. Once you start your list, you'll be surprised how easy it is to think of things because, once you've decided to get started, you'll find the ideas flow more easily as your mind gets more and more open to trying new things and in no time at all you'll have all sorts of ideas written down and you'll be well on the way to changing your life for the better.

Come on; give it a go! You've really got nothing whatsoever to lose.

4

How Soon Can I Start?

I suppose the ideal time to sit down and write your list would be December, so that you can start a whole new year with a new outlook and a clear 52 weeks in which to do all the things you'd like to. But please don't think for one minute that you have to wait that long. Starting at all is far more important than the time of year you actually do it, but I like the idea of starting the New Year with a new attitude and a whole host of things to look forward to. January and February can be incredibly dull months, let's be honest, so if you already know you've got lots of stuff to look forward to, the year will get off to the best of starts. But whenever you happen to be reading this, use it as the impetus to get your list underway, so you can begin making the most of your life.

Personally, I like to start my list in that quiet, do nothing sort of time between Christmas and New Year, when there seems to be lots of time and not a whole lot going on. I like to think of it as THE best alternative to New Year's resolutions. How many of us make those? We sit down and pledge that we will do all sorts of laudable stuff. We say next year's going to be different and we really WILL stick to our guns this time round. And then what happens? We start the year with all good intentions and find, by March, we've effectively forgotten the list exists. Someone I know calls New Year's Resolutions a "To Do List for the First Two Weeks of January" and they're not far wrong; a few months (or even weeks in some cases) into the year and the resolutions we made with such fervour such a short time earlier have fallen by the wayside. I read somewhere that for all those who join a gym in the first week of January, almost 80 per cent of them have stopped going by the third week in February.

Why is it that we give up on these things? Well, quite simply, our expectations are far greater than what we're actually capable of achieving. If we can't find the time to keep up with the ironing every week, or remember to cut the lawn on a Sunday, how the heck can we be expected to focus for long enough to read War and Peace, or learn Italian, or train to run a marathon? Please don't get me wrong, there are plenty of people out there who do these things as a matter of course, but I don't know any of them. All my friends are like me – struggling to juggle their existing commitments on a day to day basis – and they simply don't have the time or the dedication of mind to get such things done.

That's where *The 52 List* is different. It appreciates that we are all "time poor" and so it keeps things simple. You certainly don't have to wait till the end of the year to get started. If you're reading this and the New Year is still a long way off, feel free to start working on your list today. There might only be ten weeks left in the year, so you could always start your first list with just ten things. Or you can crack on with the whole 52, knowing that your list will happily take you through to the same time next year. Start on your birthday, start a *52 List* group with friends or family, start on an anniversary of a particular event, in fact, any day you like. Just start, OK?

A friend of mine, Amy decided to start a list following the funeral of her best friend, Sally, who died very suddenly in an accident at the age of 46. Amy realised that they'd been promising to get together for coffee for weeks but never got round to it, blaming work, family, children and 101 other things which were stealing their time. And then without warning, Sally was gone and there was no time left to do anything together and Amy felt this very keenly. She decided there and then that she would do everything she could to make sure that she never again sat at a friend's funeral wishing she'd got around to arranging that all important get-together and she started writing her first *52 List* the very next day.

Fortunately, not everyone is prompted by such sad circumstances but, for many, it takes an event or important milestone to spur them into action and I think that's a shame. Writing your list should be prompted by nothing more than you wanting to make your life better, more fun, much happier. It really shouldn't take a life-changing event to do that, but I understand the motivation of those that start their lists after they experience something like that and it turns their life upside down.

Life is very short, very fleeting. There's a line in the film Meet Joe Black, where Anthony Hopkins is celebrating his birthday and he says: "Sixty five years! Don't they go by in a blink?" And he's right. We never know what life will throw at us, so it's incredibly important to make the most of the time we do have. In short, it's never too early, but please don't wait till it's too late. If you've got the book now, my advice would be to start writing your List NOW. There's no time like the present, after all. Carpe diem and all that.

5

THE SERIOUS BIT

As this is ultimately a book about making the most of your life and making it better, some of you, seeing the heading of this chapter, may think "why do we have to get serious?" and, to a certain extent, you'd have a valid point, but please stick with me and I'll explain.

If we're honest, most of us would probably have to say that, overall, life isn't all that bad. It might not be all we want it to be, but at least we approach each day feeling, if not entirely happy with our lot, then at least reasonably content.

However, as part of this whole journey – which is what the book will hopefully take you on - I want to talk a bit about stress and depression, because they have unfortunately become a big part of modern life and, once you get to grips with the whole concept of *The 52 List*, you'll hopefully start to see how creating a list can be beneficial for anyone suffering from these debilitating conditions and be the first step on the road to learning to cope with them. Please don't stop reading at this point if you think that a chapter on depression has nothing to do with you. It might be far more relevant to you, or someone close to you, than you first thought.

For starters, depression is far more common than most of us realise; there are so many people who are clinically depressed and have no idea why they feel the way they do. Furthermore, although you might not think you are suffering from depression yourself, you may, after reading this chapter, realise that your friend, colleague, mother or brother is a sufferer and they don't even know it.

You might still be asking yourself why I'm so keen to raise this subject and it's simply because I was – and suppose still am – a depressive. There I said it. I am a depressive. I say "am" because I personally don't think depression is anything you can ever be totally cured of. And I say cured because it is an illness. A very real one, but one that we like to pretend doesn't exist. Unfortunately, although it's very common, depression is usually mentioned in hushed tones because we just don't feel comfortable talking about it. As a result, depression, and its many triggers and symptoms, are often ignored as people quite simply don't know how to tackle it. Talking about it embarrasses people and personally, I cannot understand why.

When I talk about depression, I'm referring to the clinical form, which is the most common. According to

Wikipedia this is "Severe, typically prolonged, feelings of despondency and dejection. A mental condition characterised by severe feelings of hopelessness and inadequacy, typically accompanied by a lack of energy and interest in life." Personally, without wanting to belittle the symptoms in the slightest, I would describe it as feeling incredibly sad for a very long time.

Less common, but far more serious in its implications is "manic depression", which is a quite different, debilitating medical condition. Manic depression — or bipolar disorder —is described, again by Wikipedia, as a major affective disorder, or mood disorder, "defined by manic or hypomanic episodes (changes from one's normal mood accompanied by high energy states)". Bipolar disorder includes clinical (or "regular") depression as a part of its diagnosis, that is to say you can't have bipolar disorder without also having clinical depression, but it's worse, far worse. The two disorders have shared similar names for many years, because they both include the component of clinical depression, but they should not be confused with each other in any way. Whereas both types of depression can be managed by medication, bipolar disorder is a condition with far more complex characteristics and will certainly need medical intervention. If, like myself, you suffer from clinical depression, you may be able to manage your condition, as I currently do, by adopting alternative ways of coping with your symptoms. This is far less likely with bipolar disorder.

Can I make it clear at this point that, whereas these descriptions are rooted in fact, the way they have been described above are my simple way to try to explain each separate condition and should not be taken as a diagnosis under any circumstances. Both can only ultimately be identified by a medical professional and, in the case of bipolar disorder, a specialist in that field. My own views and opinions should not be relied upon as a diagnosis in any way.

If, after reading this, you think you or someone close to you is suffering from depression, please, please make an appointment to talk to a doctor. Mine was so unbelievably supportive and if it weren't for him I'd still be struggling to come to terms with it to this day. There's plenty of support out there, but you need to go and seek it out. Not easy, I know – I suffered without help for over 30 years before a close friend who is a doctor suggested I see a specialist practitioner who could recognise what I was going through and offer some professional support.

It is often stated that clinical depression, and the extreme levels of stress that may give rise to it are conditions of the modern age, brought on by the fast pace at which we all seem to live our lives. It is certainly true that incidence of both types of depression is on the increase.

However, it was almost 20 years ago when a United Nations Report labelled depression as "The 20th Century Disease" and shortly thereafter, the World Health Organisation said it had become a "worldwide epidemic." So it's clearly been around longer than we think and, in reality, the origins of stress go even further back than that, way back into the depths of history.

It was the Greeks who first came to recognise the illness and actually give it a title. Derived from the Ancient Greek melas, "black", and kholé, "bile", melancholia was described by Hippocrates as a distinct condition with particular mental and physical symptoms where he stated that "fears and despondencies, if they last a long time" were symptomatic of the illness. Back in the 11th century Persian physician Avicenna described melancholia as a "depressive type of mood disorder in which the person may become suspicious and develop certain types of phobias" and that's actually quite an accurate description.

So, although we like to think that depression is a very modern thing, it's clear that the human race has been suffering from it, in its many forms, for longer than we can even imagine. I suppose it's probably because we are now much better informed and it is easier to access information that it has become more widely recognised. Unfortunately, that doesn't seem to have made suffering from it any more acceptable. It's still one of those things that we don't like to admit to and, consequently, compared to many other debilitating illnesses, there is still so little we know about it.

The result of this lack of knowledge is that, for many, depression goes un-noticed and undiagnosed; too many people suffer (literally) in silence, while those around them, not understanding the extent of their struggle are thinking they just need to "pull themselves together". I'm hoping that, after reading this chapter, you may get a better understanding of why you, or someone you know, might be feeling the way you/they do and that suffering from depression goes far deeper than just having a bad day.

I'm fairly confident that, at some time or other we've all been in the company of someone who has clearly shown all the symptoms of being mildly, or even severely depressed, and dismissed their behaviour as straightforward negativity and come to the conclusion that they just need to get a grip and be more positive. You might be surprised to know that most depressives would really like to do just that, but unfortunately, it's not that simple. Because if you're depressed you struggle to see any reason to be happy and when you feel like that, there quite often doesn't seem to be much point in doing anything.

To me, dealing with depression is a constant battle of wills; sometimes I have to make a determined effort to make myself feel better. Like many depressives, I've developed a coping mechanism. When it's good, it's very very good, but when it's bad, it's almost unbearable so, over the years, I've come up with all sorts of things I can do to stop me feeling so low.

Even when they've been sober for years, alcoholics will stand up at AA meetings and state "I am Bob and I AM an alcoholic". The capability to fall off the waggon is always there, you just have to stop yourself giving in to it. So, just as an alcoholic finds ways to stop getting drunk, depressives find ways to stop being down. And I don't mean just unhappy, or gloomy, I mean REALLY down. And what I'm ultimately hoping is that people can use the ideas in the book as tools to help them feel better about themselves and life in general. I'm hoping it will be something to turn to when things aren't going so great to perhaps give a little bit of hope and raise a few smiles.

There is no single cause of depression; if there was, I suppose it would be much simpler to come up with a solution. Different people develop it for different reasons and it has many different triggers. For some, experiencing an upsetting or stressful life event – such as bereavement, divorce, illness, redundancy and job or money worries – can be the instigator. However, it's often a combination of a number of different issues that trigger the problem.

People often talk about a "downward spiral" of events that leads to depression. For example, if your relationship with your partner breaks down, you're likely to feel low, so you stop seeing friends and family and you may start drinking more. Over a period of time, it's the combination of all of these things that make you feel even worse. What started as a feeling of being stressed and run down can then develop into something much more serious. It's estimated that around ten per cent of people suffer from depression without the trigger of a stressful event; rather it creeps up on them un-noticed as a result of low level stress maintained over a long period of time.

A great many of us will feel stressed at some part of every day; too much work, too much traffic, not enough money. In actual fact, we all need a certain amount of stress in our lives as, despite what you may think, stress can have a positive effect on us and it can help us function better as a result. Short bursts of stress can motivate you; it can increase productivity and help you achieve an incredible amount in a very short space of time. In all honesty, without the stress of a publishing deadline, I would never have completed this book! In competitive work situations, like sales, for example, there's always that desire to be better than the next guy, knowing that it really is a case of the best man (or woman) wins. It's stress that provides the adrenalin and drive that helps us succeed.

Research has shown that stress can strengthen your immune system and prevent against such diseases as

Alzheimer's, in that it keeps your brain cells working at their peak performance. Activating the reptile cortex of the brain, stress can keep you alert, motivated and ready to respond to danger. It has also been shown that patients who experience a moderate amount of stress recover faster after surgery than patients experiencing higher or lower levels of stress.

However, it's not all good news. Prolonged bouts of stress can lead to all sorts of medical problems and illness (including depression), as well as making us age much faster. So it's all about getting the balance right and making sure we don't let it overwhelm us. It needs to be treated with caution and, like most things in life, taken in moderation.

As with many experiences, we all react to stress differently. Some people live with high levels of it every day and are seemingly able to cope. However, it's equally clear that the extent to which we can cope depends entirely on the individual and the perceived, rather than actual, level of stress. For some, coping is impossible and, often before they realise it, it has taken over their everyday lives and they go from being stressed to depressed. Thankfully, it's very rare for someone to get depressed overnight, although this does happen. More usually, the progress is slow and prolonged and, because of the gradual nature of this progression, depression often goes undiagnosed.

Many don't even recognise they're suffering until they realise they can't find the energy or wherewithal to get out of bed in the morning. Then one bad day turns into two, then five and then there are no good days at all. Even positive events, such as getting married or beginning a new job, can be stressful and may lead to an episode of major depression.

Let me share a story with you. A close friend, Chris, was in a serious car accident about nine months ago. Through no fault of his own whatsoever, he was involved in a multi-car pile-up on the motorway. The driver of the car Chris hit died. So did one of the passengers. Chris broke his leg in three places and, in the weeks following the accident, had to undergo several very painful operations, including a bone graft, to repair his shattered leg. All his friends, me included, were of course very concerned. When he returned to work on crutches, everyone crowded round and offered support – help with carrying files and opening doors, getting his lunch and endless cups of tea. Chris was constantly surrounded by people who wanted to help. After two months he was back on his feet and, although he needed to get his strength back, he was physically in better shape and started to wave away the offers of practical help. However, Chris found it incredibly difficult to regain any focus after the accident. He wasn't sleeping at night, often arrived late to work and his concentration was poor.

Colleagues began talking about him behind his back, saying that he was difficult to be around, couldn't be relied on and that his work wasn't up to his usual standard They said they didn't know what was wrong with him, that he had become very uncommunicative and tricky to understand. No one wanted to work with him anymore; everyone said he was too unreliable. Before long his managers had started to question whether he was up to the job and his performance review was disappointing. He wasn't the hot shot they thought he was. And they were right, he wasn't. Because Chris was still struggling mentally months after the accident had happened and his physical injuries were healed. Suffering from a type of post-traumatic stress disorder, Chris had become severely depressed. Try as he might, he couldn't get the accident, or the people who died out of his mind. He blamed himself and found the guilt almost impossible to deal with. He was late for work because the thought of leaving the house often overwhelmed him and he just wanted to crawl back under the duvet every morning and hide from the outside world. He was very close to losing his job when, on a routine visit to his doctor, his depression was diagnosed and he started to get some help. He's not working at the moment but he is improving and hopefully, one day in the not too distant future, he'll be back to something approximating his old self.

What this highlights all too clearly is one of the biggest issues I feel we face in society as far as stress and depression are concerned; that these conditions are still very much taboo subjects. When Chris's leg was in plaster and his pain was obvious, his colleagues were falling over themselves to help him. But once the physical signs had gone, no-one thought to look any harder to find out if there was something wrong that no one could see. Unfortunately, stories similar to Chris' abound. Mental illness is, I'm afraid to say, often not regarded as a real illness at all. People are suspicious of it and many won't discuss it openly for fear of negative judgement. It's clear that there's very little acknowledgement, not just in the workplace, but in society as a whole and this really needs to change.

My own personal story is different to that of Chris' in that it wasn't triggered by any particular event, rather it built up over a considerable time. It was, over the years, described as teenage hormones, inability to adapt to new situations (going to university in my case) lack of confidence, an inferiority complex.... The list goes on and on. I reckon it all started when I was quite young and simply grew and grew until it was diagnosed in my mid-forties.

Most depressives have good days and bad days. Sometimes the bad days far outnumber all the others. Some can go for months without any sort of manifestation of it then, for no apparent reason, they seem to fall into it again – my friend Annie calls it having a "cave day" – and after a few more days, they seem to feel better. We have to acknowledge, however, that whatever way it affects them, there is no doubt that the despair they feel is very real. It might not have a visible trigger, it might be more or less severe, but there's no doubt that depression affects the sufferer tremendously and can sometimes be incredibly difficult to come to terms with.

The symptoms of depression can be complex and vary widely between individuals but, as a general rule, if you are depressed, you feel sad, hopeless and lose interest in things you used to enjoy. Other symptoms can include:

- Changes in appetite or weight
- Changes in sleeping habits
- Lack of Concentration
- Loss of energy
- Moving or speaking more slowly than usual
- Lack of motivation
- Inability to complete even the simplest of tasks
- Unexplained aches and pains
- Anger or irritability
- Bizarre or Reckless behaviour
- Self-loathing

Sufferers feel like they have a total lack of control. Even the smallest tasks – like getting up in the morning – become insurmountable and more difficult endeavours – like going to work and producing that important report – are unthinkable. Stress can often develop into depression and when that takes hold, the harder it seems to do the simplest of things which merely serves to perpetuate the feeling of lack of control and so the cycle goes on.

I think it's important to point out at this stage that this book is not, ultimately, about dealing with depression. I also need to stress that I am not an expert in this subject and that, although I've had no formal training in dealing with depression, I have suffered for many years and know all too well what it feels like. Therefore, whereas I can speak from personal experience and the amateur research I have done, this can be no substitute for seeking professional help, should you feel you are a sufferer yourself. I only know what worked for me and I know that making my own list was an important part of that, so I thought it was well worth sharing my journey to show those of you who might be struggling with day to day life that there are some simple, straight-forward ways to tackle those black days. I've also discussed *The 52 List* with a number of individuals who actually *are* experts in the field of depression, and they have seen the value in what I've done and feel that I'm probably not unique in the belief that it has given me back a sense of control. They also think that the idea of writing such a list could (and I stress the word *could*) work for a large number of depressives. I'm certainly hoping that to be the case.

Now I'm a bit of a control freak. I admit it. I'm not proud of it, but I accept it as one of my least favourite personality traits. I don't like to delegate tasks to others, I like to have everything under control, and I mean everything, all of the time. Which is, of course, totally unrealistic, so it's no wonder I get stressed! But even if you're more laid back, there's still a need to feel like you're in control of most of what goes on around you. In short, no one likes to feel they have *no* control. As life gets busier, more fast-paced and pressures of work get ever greater, it's easy to feel like it's escaping us, that we have less and less control over what happens and that we're somehow on a merry-go-round we don't have the power to slow down. The modern lives we lead are full of hassles, deadlines, frustrations, and demands. For many people, stress is so commonplace that it has become a way of life. Again, this isn't always a bad thing. In small doses, it can help you perform under pressure and motivate you to do your best. But when you're constantly running in emergency mode, your mind and body pay the price.

So if stress and depression can be caused by a feeling of lack of control, surely making small changes in your life to try to get back some of that control can only serve to lessen the symptoms? I definitely think so. Tackling the smallest of tasks and succeeding, can give a feeling of accomplishment and self-belief that can be the first step on the road to feeling better about yourself and everything around you. And this is where *The 52 List* comes in, because it's all about achieving little things that could make an enormous difference.

It's often the case that depressives don't only not care about themselves, they don't care about their surroundings either – household jobs are never done, the garden gets overgrown, dust forms piles in corners. To try to tackle this in one go would not only be foolish, but it's nigh on impossible for someone with depression to even contemplate. It's way too big and the feeling even thinking about it generates is one of uselessness and despair. But if all you had to do was fill one plant pot with soil and stick in some bulbs, or empty one drawer in the bedroom and tidy it, well that would be OK. Not easy by any means, but OK, particularly if someone helped you to do it. If you're suffering from depression, even the tiniest move in the right direction is amazing and so following a course of "little and often" is the way to go.

That's how I hope this book can help. Everything about *The 52 List* screams little and often –   to make your life better, one tiny step at a time. Not only do I hope this will help anyone suffering from depression, it can assist those supporting depressives and make *them* feel less helpless, because trying to look out for someone with depression is not at all easy. If you're currently living a very stressful life, then maybe starting a *52 List* will give you all sorts of little ways to unwind and relax and might even prevent the stress getting worse and developing into something far more serious. What I'm trying to say is, I know this isn't going to solve your problems; it's not a miracle cure. But surely it's worth a go. I'm not asking anyone to change their life significantly – that would be unrealistic. I'm just asking that you take tiny steps towards a better, more rewarding life and what could be wrong with that?

6

A WORD ABOUT LISTS

I don't know about you, but I like lists! In fact, my whole life revolves around them. When I'm working, my list of tasks helps me make sure I get everything done and not forget the important stuff. I like them outside of work too; let's be honest, we all know what happens when we go shopping without a list!

Every single one of us will make a list at some time or another –it might be a list of jobs to do, or things we want to buy, or what to pack when we go on holiday. We make birthday lists, Christmas lists…. In fact, the list of lists we all make goes on and on…

Why do we feel the need to write lists? Well, mostly, we write lists of the things we mustn't forget; lists of things we really, *really* need to do. We put them on a list to remind us, often because not doing those things will have a negative impact on our lives; the forgotten dry cleaning, the bill we didn't remember to pay, the deadline we missed. Therein lies the problem. We spend ages writing lists of things we know we *have* to do and we need to put them on a list because, if we're being truthful, they're all things we don't really *want* to do.

OK, so we all love going on holiday, but I don't know a single person who actually enjoys the process of packing, of making sure all the tickets and documents have been gathered together and that the taxi's been booked to take us to the airport. No. Didn't think so. So we make a list of all the things we need to do to actually ensure we can go on holiday because, while we're focussed on lying in the sun, we know we're not thinking about all the hoops we have to jump through to get us there.

We write lists of dull, necessary, boring, day-to-day chores (and I call them this because most of them are not exactly fun to do) because we know we have to. We know that these sort of lists contain the tasks that are nothing more than necessary evils to enable us to get to the thing we really want to be doing. No one wants to focus on these things. Therefore it's easy for our brains to ignore them, for them to slip through our thoughts like water through a sieve.

Let's go back to the idea of going on holiday. You've sat down and written the list of all the things you need to do (book the hotel and the car hire, sort the travel insurance) and the stuff you need to buy (sun cream, insect repellent, flip flops). You know you need to do all of that to make absolutely sure that nothing gets forgotten so you can have a good time when you get there. But here's a thought. How many of us sit down and write a list of the things we really want to do when we get to our destination? Places we want to go, things we want to see? Not many of us, I suspect, and why? Because we all just assume that if we get the hard stuff done and actually manage to get to wherever it is we want to go, the holiday will be brilliant because we remembered all the things we needed to do to make sure it would be. We automatically assume that once we've arrived, all the things that make a holiday perfect will just miraculously happen and we'll have a great time. But does that always happen? No, because once we get to our destination, we just want to relax and go with the flow and presume the good stuff will naturally appear because isn't that what holidays are all about, after all? OK, so I'm not like most people and I freely admit to being a list freak. So when I went to New York with my son in 2010, we sat down and wrote a list of things to do long before we got there, a list of what we wanted to do every single day. I can see some of you thinking that this might be a bit anal, but not only did it create a great sense of anticipation for months before we travelled, it also meant we got to do everything we wanted to. There was no chance of us coming back and thinking, "Oh, I wish we'd found time to go to Central Park/The Empire State Building/Grand Central Station". There was no possibility of wanting to go somewhere and it being closed, no chance of wanting to see something and finding out there were no tickets left.

Everything was planned, booked and checked before we left; nothing was left to chance. And you know what? It really was the best holiday we've ever had. It was packed full of excitement and adventure and sitting doing nothing in the sunshine. We went everywhere we wanted, we saw all the sights we were interested in, we did the lot! We planned it so carefully because after all the effort it took to get there, we didn't want to waste a single moment.

OK, so that's a holiday and not everyday life, but as far as I'm concerned, exactly the same rules should apply. If we want to do lots of good stuff, we need to get those things on a list to remind us they need to be done. That way we forget nothing and, by looking at the list, we have so much to look forward to and get excited about.

For some reason, and I've no idea why – although I'm sure there's some sort of psychological explanation out there - we always seem to think the things we don't want to do are somehow more important than the things we do want to do. As a result, we make sure we spend our time doing "necessary" stuff, but not the stuff that actually makes us happy. Take a moment to think about it. How many times have you turned down an invitation because "I've got to do the shopping/ironing/cleaning"? How many times have you missed the latest release at the cinema, or wanted to go to a play but not got round to booking the tickets. You always intended having a BBQ over the summer, but missed the one day of the year when it was sunny enough to all get out in the garden (OK, this last one might not apply to you, but I live in Manchester, so you can see where I'm coming from!)? We can all probably think of lots of occasions where we missed an opportunity to do something fun, because we felt we had to do something more "useful".

As a parent, I know that so many weekends are taken up with relatively mundane stuff. You know how it goes; you get up on Saturday morning and take number one son to football practice and youngest daughter to ballet. Then there's just time to scream around the supermarket like some demented dervish before it's time to pick them up and get them home for lunch so you can co-ordinate the rest of the day: who'll cover the swimming lessons and who's taking who to what party. You just about manage to fit in a few rushed sentences with a friend while screeching out of whichever car-park you find yourself in before going home for tea/supper, a few minutes of snatched conversation with your beloved and then bed. Well, that's just the kids, but don't try to tell me there's never been a time when you've tucked them in and not wished you were snuggled up with them, because you're quite frankly exhausted by all the endless rushing around. Then too many of us spend Saturday evening doing the ironing, or sewing names tapes into uniform and games kit or filling out all the forms for the next school trip. Or, more commonly, we simply collapse in front of the XFactor or the football or something totally mindless that we're not really interested in, but watch because we simply can't be bothered to do anything else.

Then on Sunday it's basically the same all over again, but you also have to mow the lawn or fit in a visit to grandparents ('Awwwww, do we have to?!'), there's the mountain of school uniform to be ironed, not to mention checking you've got something clean to wear yourself, so when you go to the office on Monday morning so you're not mistaken for the person on the corner selling the Big Issue. You finally fall into bed on Sunday evening shattered, emotionally drained and groaningly realising that, in a few short hours, the whole carousel of life will wiz into motion again.

OK, so maybe I'm exaggerating a bit here. Well, only a bit. Not everyone's life is like that, grant you, but I'm sure so many of you will be reading this and smiling, not happily, but wearily, nodding to yourself, admitting that it all sounds strangely familiar.

How many times have you taken the kids back to school on the first day of term and had that dreadful conversation with another parent about all the things you planned to do over the summer holidays but never seemed to find the time for? Or, how often have those of you without partners or kids (or both) bumped into a friend by the frozen pizzas and had the inevitable "Gosh, I haven't seen you in ages!" conversation? Or the "What have you been up to?", "Oh, not much" exchange? Most of us could probably look back over the last month and be hard-pushed to list more than one or two memorable events. If, by the way, you *can* do this and come up with five or six different things then you need to stop reading! Stop now! Throw the book away and get on with your life; you're doing fine! You have no need of this book or its advice and, quite frankly, you'd probably be off doing something far more fulfilling if you weren't sitting here reading this. Actually, on second thoughts, don't throw it away (recycle it at the very least). No, instead go round to a friend's for a cup of coffee and give the book to them so they can make their life as full of happiness as yours. Not wanting to assume, of course, but I bet most of you are still reading on at this stage, because everything I've said so far roughly describes your life and you really want to do something about changing it.

Life is full of lists and not very nice ones at that; very long lists of things we don't want to do, like doing the laundry and taking the cat to the vet and all sorts of other dull stuff and, to be honest, we've probably got more lists like that than we care to think about.

How about if there was a different kind list you could write? A good list. A fun list. A list that's just bursting with things you really want to do. Wouldn't that be better? I think so! *The 52 List* is an opportunity to come up with the sort of list you've probably never thought of sitting down and writing, because it's never occurred to you to write it. Why?

Because, deep down, we all assume the good stuff will happen all on its own. We all just take for granted that we'll remember the stuff we want to do simply because we want to do it, but never actually get it done because we forget the one thing we need to do more than anything else, which is to make the time to do it!

So, you're going to write a list with 52 things on it. Why 52? Because even if you only do one a week for the next year, in twelve months' time you'll have done the lot! And what makes this list so wonderful is that, because it has so many great things to do on it, you can also include a few less attractive (or even downright yucky) things, because doing them won't seem so bad when you're doing so much good stuff as well.

Now I can hear a lot of you saying, at this point, "One a week! Where on earth will I find the time? My life is too busy already, I can't possibly fit in anything else". Well, it's not that hard, believe me, you just have to know how to write the list, how to make it possible, how to finish the year with such a sense of achievement that your heart will be full. Seriously, it will! Trust me! The list I'm going to get you to write will be the best list you've ever written and the sort of list you'll never get bored of writing either. Even those of you who've never written a list in your life – although I can't possibly imagine that's going to be many – will really want to write this list this year, next year and for ever.

7

GETTING STARTED

Ever since we were small, haven't we all made lists of things we wanted to achieve? In our careers and in life. Some of us keep them in our heads, some of us write them down, but we've all been making lists for years. Big lists of big things, things that might take a lifetime to achieve, some that are just pipedreams – come on, we've all made a mental list of what we'd buy if we won the lottery, surely? – some that we might achieve, even some that, in later years, we're very glad we didn't.

So many of us expend an awful lot of time and energy thinking about the big stuff in life– like a better job, a bigger house, a faster car, an exotic holiday. Somehow we think we will be much happier if we get even one of these things, but in the whole scheme of things, does material stuff really make that much of a difference to our day to day lives? Certainly, we all want a certain standard of living, but do we really need all that to make us feel better? I think it's a problem of the modern age; I call it "the desire to acquire". Never before have we been so tempted by "the better life".

Someone I know describes it as the BBD – the Bigger, Better, Deal. We watch television and see advertisements for the latest gadget, a more expensive watch or a shiny new car. We see famous people supposedly revelling in their wealth and somehow we convince ourselves that our lives would somehow be better if we only had……….. and we come up with lists of all sorts of materialistic things we "need", because we somehow believe they will make our lives so much better.

With a few notable exceptions, here in the western world, we are the generation that really has it good. There is no fear of war (not directly, anyway), no threat of power shortages or three day weeks, no famine or disease. But somehow, that doesn't seem to be enough; we always want something better. But how much of what we think will make us happier actually costs money and lots of it? So what do we do? We work that hard to get it, that we end up spending more time at work than doing *anything* else in our lives. We get up, we go to work, we come home. Too many of us then simply flop around the house for the rest of the day and then start the same old things again the next day. We have got into the habit of not doing very much at all and it's also true that far too many of us lead incredibly sedentary lives. We need to ask ourselves if, by getting all this "stuff" we can't possibly live without, will we truly be happier, more satisfied or more fulfilled? I don't think so.

I can honestly say I'm not like that. Compared to many of my friends, I lead a very small, simple life. I don't feel the need for the fastest car or a big screen TV and I'm not really into gadgets or the latest fashion. I'm the sort of person that just wants enough – enough money to keep a roof over my head and food in the fridge and if there's anything left over, then great, I've earned a little treat. I haven't had a holiday in 4 years. I know that's far too long, but I'm not exactly suffering as a result. I'm fit and healthy and have my friends and family and you know what? I'm actually very happy with just that. I don't crave endless riches or celebrity. At this point, I can see you asking yourself why the heck I wrote this book then and it's a perfect opportunity to point out that, although it would be great if this book makes lots of money, that wasn't what motivated me to write it and, in any case, a large proportion of any revenue from its sale will be going to other people rather than into my bank account. Just in case you were wondering.

What I'm trying to say is, I think more of us would be happier with our lot in life if we stopped chasing the "Bigger Better Deal" and made more time to enjoy the small stuff. Did it ever occur to you that while you're focussing your hopes and desires on getting all those big things, your life is effectively passing you by with so many missed opportunities to enjoy the smaller pleasures that are all around you? What are you really doing with your life while you're concentrating on acquiring those big things? What about day to day, week on week? What about making the most of all the time we have while we're trying to get the big stuff done?

Think of Christmas, when all the presents are stacked around the tree. There's all sorts of packages, big and small, but how often do you find that the best presents are the ones that almost get missed? The tiny little boxes or envelopes that everyone leaves until last? A homemade gift or a card with the warmest of sentiments inside? Well that just about sums up the theory behind *The 52 List*, that the smallest things are the best. We all know the saying "the best things come in the smallest packages" and I really like that idea, so that's what I've made this book all about. Keeping it small!

What I'm trying to say is that, if you want *The 52 List* to work for you, you've got to make a shift in mind-set to realise that the big stuff isn't anywhere near as important as the small stuff. That it's the small stuff that will sustain you as you go along life's journey. I'm not saying you can't strive for the big stuff. If it's important to you then go ahead, go for it, but don't lose sight of the little things that you can do along the way to make the journey better.

If you look on the internet, you'll see thousands, yes literally thousands of lists of good things to do. They're called Bucket Lists, or "Things to Do Before You Die" or even "Things to Do Before You're 40". But when you look at the stuff that's on them, they're all generally the same in that they all take time and, more importantly, they all take money. I don't know about you but, great though it might be, I don't have the time to trek to Annapurna and I certainly don't have the money. Visiting the Taj Mahal may be inspiring, but I can't afford that either. I've come to the conclusion that these lists are only for people with time and money to spare and unfortunately, I have neither. But you know what? I don't really mind. If these are your sorts of lists, you probably think my idea is a bit small and insignificant, but I'm more than happy with my way. I often wonder what would happen if I could carry out some sort of study. Get two groups of people – one doing *The 52 List*, one group doing one of the bigger-type lists – get them to do their lists and at the end of the year, see who felt the most fulfilled. I'd bet my money on *The 52 List* group; I just know they would have more fun!

The message I really need to get across here is the need to think small. That's something we don't do very often – the message out there always seems to be "Think Big" – but then I've always liked doing things a bit differently. When it comes to writing your list you need to keep it small, keep it simple and keep it real. There are so many good things all around us, we just need to make the time to appreciate them.

Hopefully, by now you've already been doing some thinking and you've already come up with some things you want to put on your list, which is great, because it means you're already well on the way to making your life better. But before you rush off and make a start, there's some important stuff you need to know. On the basis that we're keeping it small, there's not many rules as to what should and should not be included. Please note, I say 'should' rather than 'can'; it's your list at the end of the day. There are also some things you should really do if you want to make the most of the whole experience and make those lasting memories so you need to be thinking about that too. Let me explain.......

8

THE RULES

OK, first and foremost, I know rules are boring, but I can assure you that they're really easy to follow and won't involve any sort of hardship so please just stick with me, get them out of the way and then you can get started on writing your very own *52 List*.

There might only be six rules, but every single one of them is important if you want to get your list right. They're in no particular order, so don't read anything into that, just work through them and bear them in mind as you think of things you want to put on your list.

However, I also need to point out that, if you want *The 52 List* to work properly, you must follow EVERY rule, not just some of them, or you will defeat the object and it could stop you achieving the result you want. So no cheating! Don't worry, if you feel like you're losing track as you go along, I've included a useful little summary at the end as a quick reminder.

It Has to be Achievable

I suppose I should really define this further to add "in a day or less".

We're all very time-poor. We spend most of our waking hours working, unfortunately. Then there's all the other non-work-related stuff to find time for like housework, the garden and family commitments. Phew, there's already a whole shed load of things to cram into a week, so anything else you might want to try to fit in has to be short and sweet. Well, *52 List* things are meant to be kept simple, so that shouldn't be a problem and it's why anything you put on your list has to be achievable in a day or less. Personally, I think things you can do in half a day are better. On that basis you can sometimes fit in more than one a week. Hurrah! However, some things, by their very nature, need more time, so a fair scattering of do-in-a-day things are fine. But no longer than a day. Absolutely not. Kind of defeats the object, don't you think, because I bet you've got loads of things you've wanted to do and maybe even started, but because you never finished them, they've languished for months, even years, part done. How many unfinished projects do you have lurking in the back of dusty cupboards? Too many, I suspect. So no, no more than a day to achieve each thing on your list.

This rule definitely applies to "projects", such as making or creating, because unless you commit to finishing something before you start, it's all too easy to leave it half done. Don't worry though, if you've got a really big "thing", then it can go on your list but only if you commit to splitting it down into smaller chunks which aren't necessarily reliant on each other.

Let me give you an example: a friend of mine, Jo, recently bought a house with a massive garden. The previous owner had been elderly and the garden was overgrown and almost like a jungle. Jo really wanted to get it all sorted, but as all her money had been spent on actually moving, there was little or no money left to pay anyone to do the work for her. This was a big project. Massive. Far too big to go on a *52 List* – it would clearly take months. So, we broke it down into smaller jobs, each achievable on its own, each only taking a day or less. The first thing Jo did was draw a plan of how she wanted the garden to look when it was finished (took half a day – on the list!). She then planned all the jobs she would have to do to get the garden finished – this took another half a day, so could also go on her list. Then she got started. She spent an entire Saturday chopping away all the undergrowth, another day weeding all the borders. Then she spent a day (with help from her friends) digging out a pond, which she filled with plants and fish the following week. You see where I'm going with this? Each task was complete in itself within a day. I have to be honest, Jo's whole list is probably all about the garden this year (although there are a few other things thrown in) but then this is her passion and it's what *she* wants to do, so who are we to judge? I only wish I could persuade her to spend some time in my garden instead – I'm not in the least bit green fingered.

Now I can see some of you saying that this doesn't fit the rules, because you can't put plants in your pond until you have the pond, which is strictly true, but the task of "digging out a pond" is complete in a day, as is "filling the pond with plants and fish". "Digging a pond and filling it with plants and fish" is too big a task for one day – even on the longest day of the year – so needs to be split into two.

The other things that tend to take a whole day are trips to places like beauty spots, or places of interest like museums, art galleries, or stately homes. These have to be things you can do in a day though. So, if you live in Scotland, there's no point including a trip to the Eden Project on your list UNLESS you've already booked a holiday to Cornwall, although even that's stretching it a bit. I think it's much better to focus on local attractions, because these are quite often the ones we never usually bother to investigate. We could have one of the best places of interest in the surrounding areas only a few miles down the road but never go, simply because it never occurs to us. How many of us have had conversations with people from other parts of the country (or even the world), been asked about some gallery, national park or historic building which is right on our doorstep which we have to admit to never having visited? So keep it local, within a few hours' drive. No weekends away, no overnight stays. They're more difficult to plan and cost more money and so therefore are less likely to be achieved.

It Has to be Definable

This is actually very similar to the first rule, in that the result has to be seen at the end of the day. One of the reasons we don't achieve many of the things we set out to do is that the end result often takes weeks or months to achieve. Take for example, a common New Year's Resolution to lose weight. I think we've all made that one at some stage or another but how do you measure "weight"? How do you know when you've achieved your target? And if you put a pound or two back on, have you necessarily failed? You see, it's too difficult to work out whether or not you've actually achieved your objective. Compare that, however, to "I will eat healthily for one day" which is eminently sensible and achievable. Or you could have "join the gym" on your List. I wouldn't recommend it however! Sure, the act itself is very achievable – it probably takes about 30 minutes to join – but how is joining the gym going to make your life better if you never go?

Someone I know had always wanted to read War and Peace – why they wanted to do this is beyond me, but each to their own, I suppose. When I pointed out that this was in no way suitable for a *52 List*, they said "Ah, but I'm going to read a chapter at a time and each one will be a different *52 List* item". OK, but there are 28 chapters in Book One alone! And there's 15 Books in total! Even if you read a chapter a week, you'd need seven years to read the entire thing………… and if you're not going to finish it, why on earth start? This is very different to the garden makeover above, by the way. Although digging the pond doesn't itself finish the garden, it's a complete thing in itself and can be enjoyed regardless of whether or not the rest of the garden is done. See the difference?

In a nutshell, keep long-winded, "no end in sight" stuff like this well away from your list. Stick to something you know you can do and which, more importantly, you know will make you feel happier when you've done it.

You Must be Self-Dependent

When you sit down and tell your friends and family that you're going to write a *52 List*, you can bet they will all bombard you with ideas of things you really should include, but be careful, these are things they want to do and should be reserved for their own list and not yours. Whether it's all good things or things you've been trying to put off, your list is just that – yours and yours alone. You should include stuff that's important to you, no-one else. Because at the end of the day, this is all about making **your** life better.

The other part of this rule is that anything you put on the list can't be dependent on the input of someone else to make it happen. It has to be something you can complete without relying on anyone in particular. Don't get me wrong, I'm not saying you can only include things you do on your own, far from it. *The 52 List* is all about making those around you happy as well as yourself after all and I can think of nothing worse than a picnic for a party of one. No, what I'm saying is it can't rely on anyone *specific* to get it done. You should certainly include things that you will get more fun out of if you do it with someone else, it's just that you can't define anybody by name.

I'll give you an example: "I'd like to go to on a picnic" is a great thing to put on your list, but you can't have "I want to go to on a picnic with Sue" because if Sue can't go, then you can't do it. If you invite Sue and she's free to go with you, fabulous, but by not making it too specific, you're not restricting your options or stopping yourself getting things done.

Involving your friends and those dear to you in your list is an essential part of getting the most out of it, but some things are best done on your own. My advice would be to try to include a good mix of things. You'll most probably find, as I did, that once you start involving your friends in your *52 List* things , they'll see how much fun you're having and not only will they want to be part of what you're doing, they'll be all the more keen to go off and write list of their own. Then you can get involved in the things they want to do and that could lead to so many new memories for all of you!

It Has to be Within Your Control

Whatever you put on your list, you must be able to control whether or not it actually gets done. By that I mean it can't rely on external factors, or other people for that matter, for you to be able to achieve it. I'll give you an example: you might love the ballet and if you do, but never seem to find the time to go, putting "go to the ballet" on your list is absolutely fine. However putting "go to Swan Lake when it comes to Manchester" is totally unrealistic as you have no control over which ballet is staged, or where, or when. In reality, you might knock this off your list by actually getting to go to Swan Lake in Manchester at the end of the day, but you could just as easily go to the Nutcracker in London if the opportunity arose. Either way "go to the ballet" is totally done.

This is also why you can't be specific about who you do your *52 List* stuff with. If you limit yourself to doing stuff on specific days or with specific people, you're not giving yourself enough opportunities to actually realise your ambitions and fit things into what little free time you might have. It's important to remember whose list it is and have an open mind as to when things might get done.

As I've already described in earlier chapters, it's important to retain a sense of control when it comes to your list. One of the most common symptoms of depression is a feeling of lack of control and so helping you feel like you're in control of your day to day existence is essential to keeping those unhappy feelings at bay. If anything goes wrong, how often have you felt threatened or simply frustrated by the fact that you feel you have no control over what's going on? If you want your list to work for you, you have to take control of it and make sure things are done on your terms.

It's OK to Include "Non-fun" Stuff

This is not so much a rule as just a piece of good advice and if you don't want to take it, that's fine. Some would say this is a weird one and, I suppose to a certain extent it is, but I've included it as a result of a question a friend asked me about her list at the end of last year.

Emma has been living in her "new" home for the last 18 months or so and, after the initial flurry of getting jobs done when she first moved in, there were all sorts of things she'd never got round to, like putting up a mirror and some pictures. The reason for this was simple; they just weren't urgent; all her time had been spent on getting essential jobs done – fixing a leaky roof, laying a new kitchen floor, getting new double glazing – and when all this had been finished (mostly by others who she paid to do the job) Emma had never got round to putting up those finishing touches. Hmmmmmm...... sound familiar?

Realistically, though, how long would a job like that take? An hour? Maybe two at the most. So what's the excuse? Well, quite frankly, there isn't one! Because there are all sorts of small "jobs" that are really good candidates for a *52 List* and, more importantly, should be included, for no other reason than getting them done will almost certainly make you feel better. The sort of things I'm talking about aren't the jobs we have to do, but the one's we'd do "if only we had the time" and we all know how many of those we have. Other things to consider are planting some bulbs in the garden, or putting up a shelf. Yes, they're work of a type, but the results are great. I mean, just think how good it will feel when the shelf's finally up and you can get all those books off the floor and up where they're meant to be? How good will that living room wall look when you finally put up the picture that you bought two years ago and never got round to hanging? How lovely will the garden look next spring when the bulbs you planted sprout and fill your pots and borders with colour?

You see, even though we might see them as just boring old jobs, these are the things that will make life better every day. If you're being honest, you'll admit that they take very little or no time to do, but you've never got round to because you claim there's never enough time, when what you're really saying is that you've never *made* the time. What's more, you've never thought to put them on a list either, because they're just not essential to the smooth running of your life.

I've always been a big fan of including "jobs" on a *52 List*. It never fails to make me feel really good about myself to know I'm FINALLY getting those niggly little things done and, the icing on the cake is that, because I know I've done something "practical", I never feel bad about setting time aside to do the more "fun" things on my list, like spending an afternoon at the beach or taking a few hours out on a windy afternoon to go fly a kite!

Always Keep a Record of All that You Do

I've left this rule until last, because that's where it naturally fits in, but, in actual fact, it's probably **the** most important rule of all.

We all want to have good stuff in our lives. We all want to spend time relaxing (despite how it might seem on a day-to-day basis) and doing things that we enjoy. The problem is, when we do get time to spend doing something fun, we don't often make the effort to record what we do, so we can keep the memory of it safe. How many times have you tried to recall a particular event, say a party or a wedding, and not really been able to picture what you did, or how it all looked, or what the weather was like? That's because we can only store a limited amount of information at any one time and, because we don't really give enough weight to those memories, they get lost in the soup that swirls round in our brains every day. Instead, for some strange reason, we tend only to remember what we need to do at work and whether or not there was a traffic jam on the way home from the office and all the other insignificant stuff that fills the average day. That's not a great way to be though, is it? I mean, why the heck would we want to take up valuable brain space with such nonsense? I've no idea, but we all seem to do it and, as a result, the really good stuff, the stuff that makes up happy, gets forgotten or lost somewhere in the big filing cabinet that is our mind, never to be thought of properly again. How many times have you been unable to recall when a particular event happened in your life or asked yourself when you last did a particular thing? Like when you went to such-and-such's 70th Birthday party or when you last went to the theatre? And although you try really hard to search through the grey matter, you really can't remember, because you basically didn't give enough importance to the event itself.

We often have problems with recall. However, have you noticed how much easier it becomes when someone shows us a photograph? As a general rule, we can immediately remember when it was taken. And who was there. And what time of year it was. And, most importantly, looking at the photograph almost always summons up a warm happy feeling inside as we transport ourselves back to the moment it was taken.

So do I really need to explain why this rule is so important? Probably not, as I think you've most likely got the gist of it, but I'll spell it out, just in case. Always keep a record of whatever you do on your *52 List*. No matter where you go, or what you do or who you do it with. If you go on a picnic, take photos. If you go to the theatre, keep the programme. Or the label from the bottle of champagne you drank when you watched the sunset. Or the daisies you picked when you spent the day sitting in the sunshine outside some stately home. Whatever it is that will conjure up those memories, keep it and stick it in a scrapbook.

I really can't stress this rule enough; it's vital to getting the whole concept to work as it should and, if you put it together with care, your *52 List* scrapbook could well become the most important book you ever "read". It effectively represents a year of your life after all, and it's there as a permanent reminder of the things you got up to and how you spent your time.

There's a saying out there that goes "We work to live, not live to work" but how many of us aren't really sure just how much living we actually do? We've all been there; you get together with friends you haven't seen in ages. There's so much to catch up on, so much news, so many things that must have happened since you last saw each other. However, how many times, when you ask people what they've been up to over all that time, you get the answer "Oh, nothing much" or "Nothing to write home about". Now this doesn't mean we haven't all been busy doing stuff, it's just that we haven't given any relevance to what we did do. Surely an afternoon spent looking for starfish in a rock pool or baking a cake with the kids is important? I think it is, but we might never make the time to do it and even if we do, telling someone about it isn't the same as showing them the pictures.

When everyone gets together and says "Heavens, I don't where the last year has gone", wouldn't it be great to be able to go to your bookshelves and pick up your scrapbook and realise that you know exactly where your year has gone and what you did and, what's more, you've got the pictures to prove it? Although some people – like me – might want to keep their scrapbooks just for themselves and those really close to them, you may well want to share your good times with others, because your scrapbook might not just be for your benefit. If, and only if, you're so inclined, it's for sharing with family, with friends, with your children and grandchildren, but I stress that this is only if you want to. There's nothing in *The 52 List* rules that says you have to share these memories, because it's your list after all. If you want to keep them just for you, that's fine, because they'll always be there for you, whenever you need them, whenever you need to remind yourself of all the good times you've had.

A friend of mine became a widow when she'd only been married for 10 years. When David died, Susan was just 38 and their two children were nine and seven. They don't really remember their daddy, but by sitting down and sharing her *52 List* scrapbooks, Susan could show them the small part of their lives they spent together as a family and it's helped the children build a mental picture of what David was like. The children are now in their twenties and talk about their Dad all the time – looking at all those photos and memories Susan kept for them helped them build memories of their own. I'm not saying she couldn't have done it without the scrapbook, but having it made it so much easier to make everything real for their children, who now feel able to talk about their Dad as if he'd been part of their lives for a much longer time which, in effect he was, as a result of what Susan was able to share.

Hopefully you can already see how important your *52 List* scrapbook can become and so you'll be happy to start building it from the very beginning. Personally, I think the best way to do this is as soon as possible after each event, to make sure that the memories are fresh and you truly capture the moment. Some people even like to add little handwritten notes that sum up their emotions at the time. I know that some of you will probably be joking that "updating my *52 List* Scrapbook" could be a *52 List* item on its own, but let's not even go there. Ok, I could see that working way back when we had to wait for photographs to be developed, etc., but in these days of digital photography, tablets and smartphones, there's no reason at all why you can't get it done there and then. Really, there isn't and if you start making excuses that you don't have the time, then you probably won't make the time to do the things on your list in the first place, so there'll be nothing to stick in the scrapbook!

And that's all you have to do. See, I told you the rules were easy, but as a quick reminder, here's **the low-down:**

- Keep it short – you must be able to complete each thing in a day or less
- Keep it definable – by the end of it you need to be able to see an absolute result
- Keep it to yourself – invite others to join in by all means, but each thing must be down to you to achieve
- Don't rely on things you can't control to enable you to do the things on your list
- It's good to include some "non-fun" stuff
- Keep a record

It really is that simple, but just in case you're still not sure, check out the table of what to put on the list and what to leave off and you won't go far wrong.

So, is it on the list or not..........

YES	NO
Go to the ballet	Get tickets to see Swan Lake
Visit an Art Gallery	Go to the Turner Exhibition at the Tate
Plant some bulbs	Re-design the whole garden
Re-paint the bathroom	Re-decorate the house
Put up a shelf	Take a course in DIY
Go to the beach	Learn to scuba dive
Bake a cake	Learn to bake
Have a picnic	Go on a picnic with John & Susan

And that's it! That's all you need to do, it's really not that hard. Like anything else, you just have to make the commitment to doing it and away you go.

9

LET'S GET TOGETHER...

One of the rules of *The 52 List* is that it can't be dependent on others, but a lot of people have asked me about lists for couples, so I thought it probably warranted a special mention.

Always bear in mind that the whole point of *The 52 List* is including things that YOU want to do. Now, I appreciate that you might have a significant other with similar interests and I fully understand your wish to include them as part of the experience. However, I do feel you should each make your own lists, rather than creating one together and there's some good reasons for this.

It's easy to get complacent in a relationship; to assume, quite incorrectly I have to add, that you know where you are and where you're going together, that you must necessarily have plenty of shared pastimes. Unfortunately, as I know only too well from personal experience, people can live together as a couple but have essentially separate lives and this can hide fundamental differences in personality and interests which are not necessarily highlighted on a day to day basis. Just because two people share the same space, doesn't necessarily mean they're on the same wavelength or want the same things. Additionally, we should remember that people change as the years go by and, no matter how much you had in common when you first met, who's to say you both feel the same today? As we get older, we often see new opportunities and take up an interest in something we didn't see the point of when we were younger, or decide, as time passes, that years-old, long standing interests have become a bit dull and no longer draw us in the way they used to.

My advice to you, therefore, if you are interested in writing a "couples list" is **DON'T**!

First and foremost, any list you write should be yours and yours alone, full of activities you're interested in and should never be written simply to try to please someone else. Secondly, and perhaps more significantly, creating individual lists may make you realise one of two things; either how close you are, or how far apart you've drifted.

Even assuming you're still very much thinking as one as a couple, you may still want to branch out on your own occasionally and I honestly believe the strongest relationships are those where each partner has interests that don't involve the other, but maybe that's just me? So, whereas it would be good to have some ideas you both want to try, I don't see any problem with having a total mis-match either.

What I'm trying to say is that doing things as a couple is great. But I strongly suggest you each write your own lists separately and then compare them. There may well be similarities and if you both put the same things on your lists, all well and good; that gives you a whole host of things to do together. What if you compare your lists and you find that there are no activities in common and looking at them side by side makes you realise that you and your partner have a completely different way of thinking? Fantastic! It really is, because it could give you the ideal opportunity to find out something about your partner you never knew, and so many opportunities to try new experiences together. And if your relationship has become a bit stale, just think of all the things you can start to discover and which, hopefully, will draw you together again.

10

TAKING IT TO THE NEXT LEVEL

It has to be said that I am a very lucky person indeed. My life is full of people I care for and who I know, because they tell me so, care equally for me in return. Because I'm fortunate enough to know there's always someone out there to share things with, it doesn't bother me in the slightest if I sometimes do things – like going to the cinema or wandering through the park – on my own, because I know all too well that this is my choice. But I'm very much aware of the reality that it's having the choice that makes the difference. I'm not sure whether I'd really be so keen to do things alone if that was I could ever do, if there was no one I could share things with. There's a big difference between being alone and being lonely and it's very easy to take company for granted if it's always available. If, however, you're always on your own, I can see why it might be difficult to get excited about doing the sorts of things I'm suggesting you put on your *52 List*. I'm hoping what follows will help change that.

There is no doubt that we live in a very fractured society these days. There's often little or no sense of "belonging" and a constantly shifting population makes it difficult to build any community spirit. You can test this yourself by asking yourself how well you know your neighbours and those who live near you, if you can actually admit to knowing them at all. You might even have to admit to not being able to recognise them, should they walk past you in the supermarket. That's because we don't live in small social groups any more.

However, compare this to the way we used to live. If you go back as little as two generations, life was very different. People rarely ventured very far from where they were born and they generally grew up, lived and died within an area of just a few square miles. Everybody knew everyone else locally, you knew your neighbours by name and anyone who was anyone in the local community was known to everyone. In short, everyone had someone.

Unfortunately, the same cannot be said for the world we live in today. Just nine per cent of people lived alone in 1973 but by 2011 this had risen to 16 per cent and people aged between 25 and 44 are five times more likely to be living alone than four decades ago. There is also concern that an increase in the number of people living, and essentially doing everything by themselves could correspond with a rise in social isolation and loneliness, both of which can have a significant negative impact on mental health.

All through the book, I've been stressing just how important it is to make your list all about things you want to do and how you shouldn't place any reliance on other people to help you get things done. But let's face it, we're not solitary beings and not many of us would enjoy going on a picnic on our own or just walking aimlessly along a beach with no one to share it with. Given the statistics above, it's likely that there will be a significant number of people reading this book who don't have many people in their life who they can call on when they're looking for company or something as simple as contact with another human being. Modern day life can be a very lonely existence and I know from my own experience just how sad it can make you feel. Don't despair though, hopefully *The 52 List* can act as a catalyst to start changing all that.

So if you do find yourself on your own and feeling a bit isolated, why not see writing your list as an opportunity not just to do stuff, but to get out there, make new friends and build new relationships.

Let me explain how I hope it will work by taking an example of a *52 List* item we've already suggested – going to the ballet. Suppose you're a big fan and you'd really like to go to the latest production, but you don't fancy going alone. Although you might not be able to come up with anyone to ask along, that doesn't mean there aren't plenty of people just like you, who also want to go, but equally, like you, have no one to go with. Think about it; you can't possibly be the only person who thinks going to the ballet is an enjoyable thing to do. If that was the case, theatres across the country would be startlingly empty for most, if not all, performances and no one would bother going to the trouble of putting a show together in the first place. Now imagine how many people out there might be thinking exactly the same as you; that is, really wanting to go to the ballet but not wanting to go alone. Surely there's a perfect opportunity to invite one of those people to go with you? Now I'm not suggesting for one minute that you simply start asking random people you come across if they're interested in going to the ballet, that wouldn't really be the best idea and probably not very reliable in any event. Rather I'm thinking along the lines of setting up a local group of people with common interests who might just want to help you achieve some of the things on your list and there are all sorts of ways of going about this.

In these days of social media, it's a fairly straightforward exercise to try to find out whether there are like-minded people out there. You could ask on Twitter, you could ask on Facebook; there are any number of online platforms you can use to help you find someone who thinks like you do.

If you're not into the internet, or even if you're just not that computer literate, don't worry, there are lots of other ways to find other people to connect with. Your local church hall or community centre is probably an ideal place to start, as these are often the locations where existing groups meet. If you have children, or grandchildren, try their local school. Ask if you can put something up on their notice board, or go along to one to a committee or PTA meeting and introduce yourself. It will take a little bit of effort on your part and I know it probably seems very daunting to some, but I've done it a few times in the past and have found everyone to be very friendly and welcoming. You never know who out there might be interested in getting involved.

Like everything *The 52 List* stands for, it's great to think small and my aim is to get lots of groups set up around the country, as part of a much bigger worldwide plan, to share ideas and really start making a difference. If you're still not sure how to get started, you can join in with the wider *52 List* community on Twitter and Facebook and there's the website too; you'll find all the details of these in the back of the book.

The more people get involved, the wider it will spread. Hopefully, we'll soon have *52 List* get-togethers happening all over the world!

11

And Finally...

I've loved doing *The 52 List* for the past 18 years or so. I'll hold my hands up and admit that some of those years have passed me by as far as following the rules are concerned, so when I look at my stash of scrapbooks, there are some notable omissions. I could try giving you all sorts of complicated reasons – sorry, make that excuses – as to why I never got the whole thing done every year, but if I'm honest, there's no real justification other than my own lack of motivation.

In fact, I can, in all honesty, look at every one of those years and remember why I didn't actually get my *52 List* done and you know what, I don't think it's all that important in the whole scheme of things because, since I came up with this idea all those years ago, the principles of *The 52 List* and what it's supposed to achieve have never been far from my mind. In some ways, though, I do wish I'd applied myself more and not ended up with years where I have no scrapbook to record all the seemingly unimportant events which I now can't really get into any sort of time frame.

I wish I'd done it, but I don't regret having let it pass me by, because regrets aren't something I believe in. Wishing you'd done things differently is one thing. Going forward in life burdened by regrets is never going to be recipe for happiness, so I'm a big fan of accepting that what's past is past, you cannot change it or make it better. All you can do is look to the future and take a conscious decision to make it as good as it possibly can be. So I've made a commitment to get a new list started as soon as the book is finished.

I also have to admit to never having finished several of my Lists. I own up to the fact that, even if it was only half a dozen things, there have been more than a few years when I've got to the end of December and realised that not everything got done. But you know what? That's OK too, because if I left six things undone, that means I actually did 46 wonderful things that made me happy, which was probably at least 30 more than I would've done (well, probably 40 if I'm *really* honest) had I not sat down and written a list at all.

Although YOUR *52 List* should be full of things YOU want to do, at the back of the book you'll find a whole long list of ideas that people have come up with over the years which might just help inspire you – some are seasonal, some are downright ridiculous, but they're all fabulous and fun and everything a *52 List* thing should be!

I've known for a long time that I'm not a finisher. I'm great at starting stuff, that's for sure, and maybe that's why, deep in my subconscious, I was prompted to come up with *The 52 List* at all. I think I was probably hoping it would spur me on to finish as many things as I start. In the whole scheme of things though, does it matter if I don't quite finish? No, I don't really think so. What I do know, however, is that not being good at finishing things has been the reason why this book has taken me so damn long to write and it's only the constant cajoling - OK, nagging – of certain people that's got me this far. It's also the reason why, when my deadline was getting ever nearer that I was still struggling to come up with a way to round it all off and, for once, I do have to finish this project if I want to achieve my objective. My publisher is right – there is no point whatsoever in writing a great book if you don't finish it properly. So, as I'm useless at this bit, I'm going to rely on someone else to do it for me.

I can't take any credit for what's about to follow and, after endlessly trawling the internet, I've failed to find anyone specific to credit personally, so if you're reading this and it was your imagination and creativity that came up with the words in the first place, thank you form the bottom of my heart. You've given me the perfect way to finish this book, because the sentiment sums up so perfectly what *The 52 List* is all about.

Every time you're struggling with your list, anytime you really wonder why you even started with the idea in the first place, or even if you just want to remind yourself what we're all here for, then read this; it'll help you remember what the whole point of it all is:

> "At this age, everything is changing.
> Day by day we don't notice, but just look back over the past year and you will realise everything has. People you thought that were going to be there forever aren't, and people you never imagined you'd be speaking to are now some of your closest friends.
> Life makes little sense, and the more we grow the less sense it will make. So make the most of now, before it all changes once again, because in the near future, all of this is only going to be memories."

Couldn't have put it better myself.

12

Useful Stuff

What you'll find here are all sorts of ideas for things to put on your own list, but please, don't feel you have to be restricted by this. It's purely to get that grey matter working and give you some inspiration so you can come up with a list of your own. It's been compiled from all my lists and those of my friends who have, at some time, had *52 Lists* of their own. I've divided it into sections of like-minded activities.

Please don't dismiss some of the ideas as being too vague; I've deliberately kept them this way so they appeal to the widest possible audience and are only meant as a guideline for all the things you could want to try. Equally, I bet there's lots of things you'll look at and realise you really want to do but have never actually got around to.

After that you'll find all the details of the website, the Twitter name and the Facebook page. Please feel free to go visit and join in with the conversations and post details of things you're going to do or see so they can be shared; who knows, you might inspire someone to start a list of their own.

JUST FOR FUN	
Take a walk on the beach	Get a manicure/pedicure
Go fly a kite	Row a boat
Bake a cake	Learn a poem by heart
Plant a pot of chillies on the windowsill	Spend a day without technology
Have a Seventies evening	Have a makeover
Go to a karaoke bar	Go on a nature walk
Build a sandcastle	Have lunch with a friend
Make sushi	Take a walk in the rain
Make lavender water	Learn to hula hoop
Learn a magic trick	Have a Spa Day
Go veggie for a day	Try a new recipe
Go on a picnic	Plan a movie marathon
Have a garden party	Buy a hat
Go on a falconry day	Wear a hat
Have a day without television	Write a letter to an old friend
Make bread	Play in the snow
Organise a dinner safari *	Have an indoor picnic
Have a BBQ	Go to a Tea Dance
Make novelty ice cubes	Go on a family bike ride
Plan a romantic evening for two	Throw a Christmas party in June
Go on a family bike ride	Do a Bungee Jump
Do a 100 piece jigsaw	Go parasailing

* Everyone cooks a different course and you walk from house to house, eating as you go.

DAYS OUT	
Stately homes	Journey on a steam train
Water Parks	Storm a castle
Nature Reserves	Go down a cave
Woodlands	Do a zipwire challenge
Mountains	Go bowling
Beaches	Go to a food festival
National Parks	Pitch a tent in the park
Theme Parks	Have a teddy bears' picnic
National Monuments	Go to a farmers market
Parks and Gardens	A day at the zoo
Historic Buildings	Berry picking
Ride on public transport for a day	

HOMES & GARDENS	
Put up a swing	Plant some bulbs
Have a clothes-swap party	Put up a shelf
Clean the window blinds	Decorate a room
Build a BBQ	Dig a pond
Put up a bird box	Plant a herb garden
Re-arrange the furniture	Plant a vegetable garden
Make a bee hotel	Build a rockery
Plant a tree	Hang some pictures
Have a garage sale	

A BIT OF CULTURE	
An art gallery	Concerts/Live Music Event
A play	Wine tasting
The opera	Comedy Club
Open air installations	Hold a Burns Night Supper
The ballet	Poetry readings
Vintage cinema	Wander round the library
Any kind of cinema	Open mic night

PRACTICALITIES	
Clean behind all the appliances	Learn how to change a tyre on the car
Wash the windows	Paint the front door
Decorate the bathroom	Clear out your wardrobe
Fix a Squeaky door	Sort the "man drawer" **
Tidy the garage	Clear out your make up drawer
Review household expenses	Empty your old email folders

** The drawer in your house, usually in the kitchen, where you
    keep all sorts of useless rubbish like old batteries, rubber
    bands, spare fuses, keys to locks you no longer have, and
    so on. Courtesy of Michael Macintyre

GETTING CRAFTY	
Burn a CD of your favourite songs	Build a time capsule & bury in the garden
Create a wish tree for Christmas	Make something out of clay
Make a homemade card	Build a scarecrow
Carve a pumpkin	Sew a beach bag
Make homemade soap	Paint a pot
Make a photo collage	Tie dye a t-shirt
Make a cushion	Paint a picture
Create a decoupage frame	Make friendship bracelets
Make Jam	

Links

 Follow us on Twitter @The52List

 Like us on Facebook at The 52 List

Visit our website: www.the52list.com

The following two sites are run by national charities and have some great ideas on ways to deal with mental illness, stress and depression:

Rethink Mental Illness: www.rethink.org

Time To Change: www.time-to-change.org.uk

Susan Leigh is a registered counsellor and hypnotherapist and has been invaluable in the whole *52 List* project. Her website is full of helpful tips on coping with stress:

Live Life Well: www.lifestyletherapy.net